To Judy & Bob -
a good read!
Nancy Susan Michael

# Tinkering Around With Insanity

by

Nancy Susan Michael

authorHOUSE

*1663 LIBERTY DRIVE, SUITE 200*
*BLOOMINGTON, INDIANA 47403*
*(800) 839-8640*
*www.authorhouse.com*

© 2004 Nancy Susan Michael
All Rights Reserved.

No part of this book may be reproduced, stored in a retrieval system, or transmitted by any means without the written permission of the author.

First published by AuthorHouse 05/19/04

ISBN: 1-4184-1968-0 (e)
ISBN: 1-4184-1967-2 (sc)
ISBN: 1-4184-1966-4 (dj)


Library of Congress Control Number: 2004093635

Printed in the United States of America
Bloomington, Indiana

This book is printed on acid-free paper.

# Table of Contents

| | |
|---|---:|
| An Unbridled Passion | 1 |
| What Is Poetry | 7 |
| Love n' Stuff | 8 |
| You and Me | 12 |
| For The Wise | 14 |
| Christmas is for Children | 15 |
| Christmas Love Begins | 16 |
| Time To Repent | 17 |
| A Christmas Roast | 18 |
| Recipe of the Day | 19 |
| What's Going On | 22 |
| God Love Us | 24 |
| Only I | 26 |
| A Boiling Point | 28 |
| Summer's Night Eve | 30 |
| Self-Expression | 36 |
| Death and Reality | 38 |
| That Extra Mile | 39 |
| Best By Far | 40 |
| In this Corner | 41 |
| Reaching Towards Space | 43 |
| It's All Over | 47 |
| Approving the New Year | 53 |
| Awaken Your Senses | 56 |
| A Song In Your Heart | 58 |

| | |
|---|---|
| Twist of Luck | 59 |
| What You Mean to Me | 60 |
| The Power of Forgiveness | 62 |
| In my Power | 64 |
| Death by Consciousness | 67 |
| On a Journey of Love | 69 |
| Forever Lost in Love | 70 |
| A Fantasy Ride | 72 |
| A Parkinson's Love | 74 |
| Monsters and Demons | 77 |
| The Last Train | 81 |
| Way Back When | 84 |
| A Winged Flight | 85 |
| My Only One | 89 |
| In A Way | 90 |
| Oh I Pray | 91 |
| Beauty In The Beholder | 92 |
| Best In Life | 94 |
| Whispers of Roses | 96 |
| Spare the Lonely | 99 |
| Stronger Than Ever | 102 |
| Looking For A Pardon | 103 |
| Hearts of Many | 106 |
| Within My Grasp | 108 |
| A Way Of Meaning | 110 |
| In The Darkness | 114 |
| A Guiding Vision | 117 |

*Tinkering Around With Insanity*

# An Unbridled Passion

When my heart pours forth,
it means quite possibly,
that I'm in love with you.
I know you feel it too.
Just by the way you look at me.
It is so comfy to lay next to you.
I spend some very lonely nights,
missing you greatly.
I keep wishing you were here with me,
As I pretend to sing,
the scale of how much I love thee,
It is in my dreams,
that I lay next to you,
till the time comes,
when my arms reach out for you.
I can take all your worries,
away from you for just a moment.
When I may be in that special heaven.
It will be selective,
no doubt about it,
as I see fit.
I can only see,
to be with you,
on a rainy day.
I could count the raindrops,
till I can be with you.
Even the sun shines,
up in the sky,

*Nancy Susan Michael*

just for you.
Even the stars twinkle,
just enough to be noticed,
for you and me.
I take it where we are,
on the fair way of life,
about ready to enter,
a new special day,
when we are in love,
it is a great thing.
A new day it can bring.
Adventures good or bad,
to help fan the flames of romance,
burning so bright.
As I reach out for you,
you are on my mind,
during the day and night time too.
We have the type of romance,
which strengthen the ties that bind us.
We're about ready to enter,
a new special day.
When we are in love,
it is a great thing,
for each new day can bring,
adventures good or bad.
Will help to fan the flames of
romance.
Burning so bright.
As I reach out for you,
you are on my mind,
during the day and nighttime too.

*Tinkering Around With Insanity*

All I need to do is,
to put things into proper perspective,
to belying next to you in bed.
This is where I belong.
Every hour on the hour I think of you.
Not a day goes by,
that I don't call for you.
You so gallantly sweep me off my feet.
A nervous twitch,
creeps in my life.
You see me on the rise,
so gallantly,
you are there to catch me,
when I fall.
You always aim to please!
You help me out of the doldrums
or bring me out of the clouds,
into our unsuspecting arms.
I so neatly fly.
That's when your charms take over.
You always have a way satisfying
me 100%.
I know the best spot to be romantically.
If it's romance I'm looking for,
you are all I want,
in bed and out of bed.
If it's romance I'm looking for,
I want all of you and I want more
more and more,
In order just to show you,
what we have between us,
It is ever lasting love.

*Nancy Susan Michael*

It is a true trip that two
souls are taking,
It is on we are making,
just for ourselves.
I see a trip for two,
it is just for ourselves,
To enjoy,
with nobody else to interfere...
Even as I hold you near,
even in a safe and quiet spot,
people can always run interference
in our lives,
even when they aren't around,
they can make our lives miserable.
This delicate flower of romance and love,
has the ability to resist outside interference,
even in a safe and quiet spot.
They can sometimes make or break,
the sensitive foundation of love.
It is within the glory,
that we can reach the pinnacle,
of love itself.
With such rapture that our love has,
what we do when we're together,
we can tell our love is reaching a pinnacle,
of love in itself.
We can always make it on the double!
Like two strong lightening bolts,
up in the sky,
I see nothing but a love so true,
That when I said I do,
I meant forever...

*Tinkering Around With Insanity*

I am so hopelessly in love with you.
Always will be till the end of time.
I know that's a good sign,
to want to be closer together.
For love says it all,
like unbridled passion,
it gets out of control.
It is like two wild steeds,
galloping across the hillsides,
It further cements our love together,
in a wild sort of way.
It is when east meets west.
It is such an uncontrollable passion.
We make a mad dash for each other.
Just to be together.
Our love is like a seed to be planted.
when planted it sprouts roots
then it decides to grow and grow...
It keeps on reaching for the sky.
Your love I will cherish over and over for
every waking hour.
If it were within my power,
I would give everybody a love
just like ours.
Just to show them what kind of stuff
we're made of...
So the next time you think of us,
watch the fury and unbridled passion of a
group of wild horses together...
yes mamn' it's that wild
and uncontrolled...

*Nancy Susan Michael*

Remember me and Alan,
like sands through the hour glass of time,
within time our love has,
grown and grown...
To conquer any task at hand,
all I need to do is thank God for a
love like ours.
I could only love you more and more,
with each passing moment,
so I say God bless you Alan...
so our love isn't half bad!!!

# What Is Poetry

If brought to foreign countries,
it would have to learn the language.
If just chock full of inspiration and love,
It has had a visit from God.
If poetry did smile just for you,
you must have found a four-leaf clover.
If poetry complains,
it will always be liked by someone.
If poetry is funny,
laughter cures all.
If poetry is noticed,
a new star is born.
If poetry prays for peace,
it will get liberty and justice
for all.
If the poetry finds love,
it will be shown love.
If poetry is shown indifference,
it will be shown the truth
& the way of God.
If all this gives Poetry a smile,
then this makes me a very happy Poet!

*Nancy Susan Michael*

# Love n' Stuff

First it begins in the
galaxies,
high above the earth,
there comes a moment when
a single thought transpires across the
heavens.
This single thought
traveling through this vast land,
where God is known to reside.
First we check to see
just what this single thought
is thinking,
for that is the most important
thing,
is what does this single thought
want?
This single thought surpasses
it lands in a shield,
a protective body,
then the thought is nourished,
beyond belief than anyone had seen.
It has found what we call life,
and in life we must pour
an unknown substance called
"Life and love"
When this unknown entity or soul,
reaches this state,
it hits a plateau,
where it grabs at life,

*Tinkering Around With Insanity*

and makes a go of it.
Then this entity goes through
different stages,
whereas this is call
mankind and living life to
it's fullest.
This entity unbeknownst to
everyone,
the cent which holds this
entity inside its host,
is called love and the sheer
spirit in which it is held,
keeps this entity alive
and nourished for a long time.
It is it's sheer impact
upon the world,
which makes a difference is
how this spirit or entity
manages to survive.
This is how we have the will
in us to survive,
plus this other unknown
entity who has stepped in,
God.
Once life is a given,
it must work hard to survive,
the rest of what we call "Life."
And the will to survive,
is the biggest power more than
anything I believe it to be.
Let us examine the factors in
this heavenly body or mass

called "creatures of God."
To at least function,
these creatures of life,
called a result of God's
love or planning,
have created these creations,
which believe in the Lord
Almighty.
With presiding over them,
they reproduce,
making new entities of life.
There is a sad note
to this living entity,
it is called "War."
There are many things which this
entity can go through,
it can be war with himself,
or war on the physical plane
or reality.
You take three single entities,
putting them together
believe it or not can work
out.
It depends upon the time in
which the soul or
entity in time hit the
body in which it resides,
depends upon or not on how
we get along as human beings.

*Tinkering Around With Insanity*

I believe, Alan, that we met at the
right time and place,
and our bodies "mesh" together
well in a single, voluntary act
from God,
in a thing that we call
love,
which we borrowed from God!
Which will never die,
we are blessed!

*Nancy Susan Michael*

# You and Me

In time and space,
we begin to see,
what our elders left,
for us were you and me.
When you were born,
you were born with a silver spoon.
When me was born,
all dad could do was croon.
For ol' times sake,
I sat on daddy's lap.
Now I have a heart.
Dad made a baby girl.
He said I'd give him no crap,
so I gave it a whirl.
Life that is.
I'd do the best I could,
to show that brother of mine,
just what love meant.
Even if I got a bit out of line,
you were always there brother,
to lend a helping hand.
When I was just a toddler,
from my dad I'd run.
My butt turned pink,
when my dad use to paddle.
He'd use the back of the shoe trick,
it taught me how to waddle.

*Tinkering Around With Insanity*

His morning cereal I'd throw in the sink.
We use to have these food fights,
but he'd do it first.
Our of crime I'd take a bite,
just to have those food fights.
It was a must,
it was quite a sight,
that they should fuss,
over me.
To improve my eyesight,
realizing nothing is free
in this life.
It's been a struggle to the end.
May all the brothers and sisters,
have fun in this world.
Let life's forces be with you,
brother you're all right in my book,
and love you lots
too!

*Nancy Susan Michael*

# For The Wise

Christmas is said,
to be for the moment.
For it isn't a prize your got,
it is an understanding of God.
When going to church,
during the holiday season,
you are going to pray to God.
For what it means to you,
to be in church that day.
Just sitting and praying,
to the Lord above.
To thank him for what you have.
To see through any problem,
that you may have.
To pray for family and friends,
whom you've known a long time.
To give a toast,
to family members at Christmas.
To indulge in reading the family bible.
To praise God that there is a Christmas.
That you are thankful to be alive!

# Christmas is for Children

As Christmas is yet to come,
preparations are in order.
A mouse may not even stir.
The children are out front,
the storm we got the brunt.
The children are outside,
building a snowman.
The lights are all over,
it is cold outside – brrrr!
There are cookies left for Santa.
As goes the songs,
Santa made his visit.
The time sure flies.
Here it is New Years Day.
The children have their say.
On Christmas day.
They will pray on Christmas day,
we'll make a decision,
to have the whole family over,
just for Christmas dinner!

*Nancy Susan Michael*

# Christmas Love Begins

Christmas love begins,
just by picking up the bible.
Praying to God earnestly.
It means going to church to see,
just what Christmas is all about.
It is for the moment,
where has the time gone?
Since we have made a commitment to God.
That we are thankful for
what we have.
It is the singing of Christmas carols.
It is the wrapping of Christmas gifts.
It is the remembering of folks,
it is standing by the window,
watching the snow fall.
It is sitting by a fireplace,
watching the children build a snowman.
It is going for the sleigh ride in the snow.

## Time To Repent

The Christmas holidays are upon us.
We will see that everyone is remembered,
around Christmas time.
It is a time to be thankful,
for everything that we have.
It's a time to be present.
When you acknowledge that
Jesus Christ was born on this day.
Christmas carolers are singing.
Amazing Grace permeates the air.
It is time to give penance.
To what we are thankful for.
It's time to realize that there is a God.
It is time to carry the bible with you.
Seeing your way through tough problems,
that you may have created,
throughout the year.
It is time to believe in yourself!

*Nancy Susan Michael*

# A Christmas Roast

I will most definitely be there for Christmas
holiday.
When you smell that turkey dinner,
starting to cook in the oven.
It will be the apple cider,
that is poured into celebration.
It's the turkey roasting over an open fire.
It is chestnuts hanging
on the Christmas tree.
It is the brightly colored packages,
sitting under the Christmas tree.
It is the children,
running down the stairs,
to see what they got for Christmas.
It is the mistletoe,
hanging at the door.
It is stealing a kiss.
With the best interest at heart.
It is saying prayers for your loved ones,
just to keep them safe.
All this adds to the holiday cheer!

## Recipe of the Day

I thought I would write,
a grand poem just for you.
I'd create quite a sight,
just trying to please you too.
For that one alone is hard to do.
When you're trying to please,
the whole world,
you throw in a dash of love,
something you can taste.
A pinch of what you can have,
the good word a day.
To wipe away a tear,
you could add a dash of kindness.
Even though there is less,
of what we want to have.
They say the world is your oyster,
why not give it a whirl?
Use this recipe instead of one for food,
a smile can work wonders.
It can put you in the mood.
A loving couple,
will hang a sign on the door.
Do not disturb.
Love has found its way.
It may permanently stay.
No matter what the word.
A sigh is worth a thousand words.
How to meet a demanding day.
Add encouragement when needed.

*Nancy Susan Michael*

To enrich our consciousness.
It will help a few.
To just show a dash of gratitude,
to see the improvement will be soon.
Your recipe should be fully blessed.
Even with a small amount of concern.
You can carry it to full term.
With lots of energy to burn.
It is just one of those things,
we wait to see what each day brings.
Its "hats-off" to the one fellow,
who finds the right recipe for World Love.
It is what we seek about in life,
shows others what we like.
Spreading it miles wide,
others will take your side.
Putting out the same recipe.
The old adage still works the best,
especially if it stands out among
all the rest.
We will try to remove hate,
give us some space.
In order to remove it,
you sweeten hate with love.
It works all the time.
A quick wave and smile,
will do the trick.
There may be many ways in
which to sooth the savage beast.
The recipe to him should contain,
a lot of love in any form.

*Tinkering Around With Insanity*

From you or me,
from God up above,
on earth peace would reign.
The white dove.
We sit and ponder once more,
asking ourselves whatever for?
It will be that I do,
something different.
It will be time well spent too.
Sharing it with just what
this poems recipe needs
to make it pay.
For this poem can only help those in love,
only this poem can have its say!

*Nancy Susan Michael*

# What's Going On

It is my pleasure,
to start the day off new.
It may even surprise you,
and calm yourself to sleep.
It is forgotten in your mind.
There is even a possibility
of a visit from another century.
There is a possibility of a rebirth.
Into a single mind emersion.
Into the gray matter it shall seep,
forming into an ideal for the day.
It will then circulate around,
picking up other ideas.
The ideas permeate the air waves,
then slipped into realities.
Becoming part of society.
It will be on a grand scale.
In its fleeting moment.
To seek the approval of others.
It will be on a scale of fantastic.
It being then will not be enough.
It shall be given a true color.
To be presented in this form.
It shall be over seen by less.
In some form of mass genealogy.
It will be of sound mind.
To perform on an equal basis.
It shall have spirit and soul.
Being sought by others.

*Tinkering Around With Insanity*

It shall always be remembered.
A single molecule could change
its entire form, shape and entity.
To be believed in some form,
shall be executed immediately.
Being a part of society.
Being accepted as the mainstream
of America.
The multitude will run for cover.
If the presentation is all wrong,
to see the future is believable
when the multitudes gather.
The puzzle piece fits just right,
into the scheming of others.
If it doesn't fit just so,
others shall smile gleefully,
to make the presentation just so.
For everyone has a say-so,
in this miraculous happening.
There is always that possibility,
that you may go down
in shining glory.
Ebbed into the formation of the soul.
Best believed and remembered by all,
was that single idea that
fell into the waiting hands of society.
Just fresh from the corner stones
of our mind!

*Nancy Susan Michael*

# God Love Us

God love us till we die,
we sometimes don't think you're there.
We hang our heads and sigh,
nothing in life seems fair.
Without you, God, we lose our way,
on this earth we dare stay.
We lose all sense of what's right,
we go fight battles that don't seem right.
Then we turn to God in prayer.
Dear Lord, if we have an ax to grind
we come to you.
There are many such strange things
you make us do.
It is remarkable how much better
we feel,
when we come to you.
We bend our knees in solemn prayers,
decide to fight against evil,
those who have no say.
In this world full of good and bad,
we set our own sights.
This way we haven't been had.
Realistically, our faults are of our own,
many needless things we have sewn.
There is much proof that God is surrounding
you,
with his raptured love.
That no matter what you've done in life,
you can always be forgiven.

*Tinkering Around With Insanity*

No matter what is said between you
and the Lord,
it better be well spoken.
For it is only a token,
a part of you,
that needs to be forgiven which
is your soul.
As we get closer and closer to heaven,
we can sit with a smile.
Rest assured that God will judge us all.
So no matter what race or color or what
we've done,
God will see us all!

*Nancy Susan Michael*

# Only I

Only I
can give you such outreaching love,
as it can go to the inner depths of our souls.
It can bring us a treasure trough,
of memories savored,
time can take its toll.
We won't let it do that,
we'll stand tall,
under it all,
no matter what it means.
There is no place I'd rather be, dear,
that under the covers hugging you near.
With you reaching out for me,
I can see your innermost beauty,
as you show me rapture from deep inside.
The love is what is written on your face.
You put my heart through all its paces...
those wonderful feelings race up and down
my spine.
You're love I can only hope to give you,
as much as you give me...
I owe you a wonderful lifetime of love,
set up in a different way.
I so wish my body didn't have
Parkinson's Disease,
where I start and stop,
for I'd love the hell out of you,
if I only could till I dropped.

## *Tinkering Around With Insanity*

I would go to the ends of the earth,
just to please you.
If there's anything I can do,
only if anything to prove
how very much you're loved.
As I go on my lonely sojourn,
I again take my turn,
just to prove how much I love him.
The look of love is in your eyes,
everytime you look at me.
As I sit in my doldrums,
pondering over my inadequacies,
I don't overlook any of them.
For I have many needless to say.
It is time now for me to count my blessings.
The hard reality of it all is,
for I cannot stop pause,
for even a brief moment.
There is much action going on
that I don't know about.
I want us never to part,
if only I had a different start.
It would be me trying to please you,
for I'd be a real fool,
if I were to ever let you go!!

*Nancy Susan Michael*

# A Boiling Point

You reach a boiling point when,
your memories out of line,
you seem to keep on going,
even lately when you been showing'
those aging wrinkle likes of Father Time.
You just don't seem to shine,
yesterday took it all out of you.
You aren't type to be pushy,
but you will to help someone out.
Occasionally when your temper gets hot,
you'll turn quickly into a water spout.
On red you'll be green with envy,
around corners you won't dilly dally…
Even if your companion is
that silly, voluptuous, cell phone crazy
blonde called Sally.
Watch out for her if she is in your way,
for even the best have collapsed at the
sight of her.
Stigmatized for life she is a classy chick,
who will willingly burn both candles,
down to the wick.
There is always one of these,
out on the open road,
who never bother to phone home.
The way she moves it makes the biggest men,
weep, cry and moan,
some of them their eyes get wide,
at the sight of her contour lines they just groan.

### *Tinkering Around With Insanity*

Sally won't get very much mileage
out on the open highway,
mileage is not a concern to her.
She always like to create a stir,
with her style, fashion and flair...
Why she doesn't even mind if other's stare.
Around corners she'll zip,
with such grace and ease,
since being blonde in color,
she's a bit of a tease.
She'll always toot her own horn,
she was just built that way...
Being stuck up and snobbish,
is not her forte.
Being a showoff she'll always be,
for she was just built that way.
In case you didn't know it,
she runs on just pennies,
she can stop on a dime
obey your every command.
She won't stand to be dammed.
Her lure will get the biggest catch,
the one with the most money,
for out there in car dealership land,
everybody will be her honey!

*Nancy Susan Michael*

# Summer's Night Eve

Yo' listen my friends and
you shall hear,
maybe written in these
pages of fear.
You will hear of yourself
in three D.
Getting ready for a midnight
jaunt,
as you head out for your
favorite haunt.
As you get into your red XKE,
you quickly open the
door to see,
your heart spilled forth you
shot a smile filled
with glee.
Right next door to the driver's
seat,
your wildest dreams oh what
a treat.
Sat the biggest, bosomed, blonde
that you ever did see.
Then it came upon this fellow,
whose shocked look turned
to mellow.
Then he sputtered,
'where did you come from?'
'How'd you get into my car,'
he asked much to his

## Tinkering Around With Insanity

chagrin.
Looking at her had to be
a cardinal sin.
She flashed him a sheepish grin,
that was a mile wide.
She cleared her throat choking
as she still sat inside.
The fellow sat next to her
moping,
wondering just what to do next.
The first words came out
of the blonde,
as she cleared her throat
choking.
'You don't remember the night
before,'
'you went for the round robin
and kept wanting more,'
'so the drunker you got
the more you forgot,
so I charged you an arm
and a leg.
That threw the fellow into
total shock,
hard to take the whole situation
into stock.
As he got a bit bolder,
he saw his work folder,
on the floor beside her feet.
The blonde was use to liability,
but that was the fellow's
reality.

*Nancy Susan Michael*

He stuck his hand into his pocket,
he searched for his keys in-
stead pulled out a locket.
The blond spoke,
'Since you maxed all your cards and
wanted more,
the story will get more sordid.'
'Equal time equal payment' the
blonde repeated,
'to get your XKE back you signed
to me an IOU.'
The fellow sank back in defeat,
but then he looked at her
again,
and decided not to retreat.
It looked like she was
worth it,
a little too hard to resist.
So begrudgingly he took
the car keys from her
and asked where she wanted to go.
In her weakest voice ever
she said 'home,' form which
she won't too far roam.
He got the car started and
out of the garage,
when heavy rain poured or it
must have been a mirage.
Either way the fellow did not
drive in a straight line.
She told tales of
her sojourns,

*Tinkering Around With Insanity*

and went along for the ride.
She looked at him drunkedly
and asked 'where are you going?'
I'm not going to work for
I got fired the night before.'
'That is my folder you have
there on the floor.'
Suddenly he heard a flop, flop, flop,
yes, he had a flat tire and
had to stop.
Out of the car he got,
just to see the rain come down
hard in spots.
'By the way', said the blonde,
'you met me at the golf course,
at hole number 10 par 5.'
As he fixed his flat tire,
a mental picture flashed through
his mind as to what happened the day before.
He just sat down and started to
cry.
Oh what a big surprise!
The blonde started choking and
up came the drinks from
the day before,
all over his car a real
great eyesore.
She said she didn't mind living
with foreclosure,
knowing him was a real dunce all
over.

*Nancy Susan Michael*

The blonde decided the night
before,
a joint venture was for them
in store.
With style and flair,
he turned his car back on,
blinking because of the sun's glare.
The name of his local haunt
came to mind,
said he wanted to get drunk
till he got the bends.
After which his memory he did lend.
This was more of a case when,
no matter what the heck he did.
They took a joint vote and decided
to go to Vegas,
where they could pass many a buck.
As they pulled into Vegas
they found a place to stay.
They found room to stay.
When they awoke the next day
the fellow found a lucky streak.
In his wildest dreams ever,
his body started to tremble...
As the blonde sat up on the table,
she did her thing,
just for the fellow she exposed
her knees.
In that day and age it
was heard of!
She even caused a small scuffle.

*Tinkering Around With Insanity*

She won her fellow a lot of money,
then he took to calling her honey.
They took Vegas by storm,
they didn't look the least war-torn.
The next day they purchased rings,
and he bought her a gown.
Then in Vegas looking for a chapel
they made the rounds.
They found a chapel with the name
'I got lucky'.
Even though he had a few million bucks,
he married her to get his life
out of a rut.
When he woke up with his bride
the next morning still drinking wine,
he saw her for the first time as she
really was and choked.
She looked just like the "Bride
of Frankenstein!"
A case of mistaken identity.
Oh what a poor, pitiful case
was he,
for the whole world to see.
After she removed all her makeup,
so that he could see,
just what really was his reality!

*Nancy Susan Michael*

# Self-Expression

Poetry is just a form of self-expression,
of telling someone how much they
are loved not to mention,
the fact that they are idolized,
with all my heart I surmise,
it is quite clear that I love you and
you love me.
There is a lot of power behind those
words and send a soft breeze,
over any valley of dissension to
correct what's wrong.
So nothing has out of
a relationship gone.
There is strength in those three words that
have been put into songs.
I love you beats with a strong
wonderful pulse for any couple.
When the angry feather's
have been ruffled,
it is like compared to something
sweet to eat.
It tastes good and can't be beat.
Well the old words 'I love you' can set
many emotions flowing.
It gets that inner clock to going,
where there is no stopping the flowing
of sensations that pour forth.

*Tinkering Around With Insanity*

It is from my own
knowledge and source...
that when two people in love
endorse,
their own signature to the words
I love you by saying,
and perhaps also praying,
can help these words to mend a broken heart
it goes without saying.
So in the honor or love and romance,
a couple can always give it a second chance.
With this form of self-expression of the heart,
when used often they will never part!

*Nancy Susan Michael*

# Death and Reality

## Dedicated to my battle with Parkinson's

Death is reality no matter what.
It is still there,
in all it's elaborate trappings.
Unlike a gift and all it's wrappings.
Unwrap one piece at a time.
Such as the bow and paper.
This is the equivalent of with what
you meet death with.
The final passing on will happen,
so unwrap your gift carefully.
As removing one symptom
after another.
We can maintain perspective.
From God that springs forth
from death.
Life will go on living,
death dies away!

*Tinkering Around With Insanity*

# That Extra Mile

That extra mile you can go.
For someone near and dear,
can cause tears and fall.
Before the small
things let you down.
Before you get left behind,
society has let your heart,
go the extra mile.
Then look it up again.
When your heart is on the mend,
you'll find yourself getting
down again.
It is the latest fashion trend,
to be on the receiving end!

*Nancy Susan Michael*

# Best By Far

A right way to say hello,
if you take it nice and slow.
For it is the way in which,
your lips part to express it.
That is the best way to live,
the candle burned at both
ends will not,
keep away your tears or add
to your fears.
A smile will be ruined by
this lack of sleep.
A perfectly good smile,
makes it worth all the while.
It will be up to you to prove,
that a good smile says it all.
It can make your world go around,
let no one put you down!

## In this Corner

In this corner what do we have,
nothing but handy wipes and suave.
It is always good for a laugh,
we don't pretend to be daft.
What we have in this corner,
it won't win any money.
It won't call you honey.
You can take the lead,
if you believe in Stephen King.
Edgar Allen Poe is great.
A great name he did make...
If you can see your way through
you'll be out of that corner,
you won't either be a fool.
You'll be in center stage of life,
being more than just polite.
You'll see your ring announcer,
encouraging you all the way.
You can stay in one corner in life,
or set your goals our of sight.
It's a boxer's dream,
to be the champion of the world,
for it isn't any kind of scheme,
that you chose this to do,
with a smile on your face.
As you pursue your goal in hand,
you may jump around before you land,
that perfect nitch in life.

*Nancy Susan Michael*

You can punch your way,
through any adversities.
You can always make it worst,
by stepping around or the issues you
skirt.
Once in life you hear that bell,
sound off in the distance,
it has the right to make you tense.
It's not there to make you tense.
It's not there to make you well,
but to warn you life is almost over.
Since things are almost over,
we jump around more,
punching at everything we see,
trying to make a score.
When it comes that time in life,
we have no more crosses to burn.
We must lay down our boxing gloves,
when the referee blows that whistle,
we can no more shove.
In the end of life there is always a winner,
someone wins a medal and money.
What a fine sport boxing is,
it shows perseverance,
blood, sweat and tears.
For if we didn't have these qualities,
we could never fight our way through
life,
only expecting the best in life that
can BE!

*Tinkering Around With Insanity*

# Reaching Towards Space

It is apparent to me that,
in spite of the fact you put your
foot in your mouth,
after
becoming involved in a spat.
I get to wake up and explore the inner
conveniences of your mind.
You've driven a long ways just to be
there.
The Marshland sprinkled with dew,
shines brightly.
You have another chance to explore.
As you check in for another progress
report,
they ask you if you would like to be
there.
'Yes' to which you reply eagerly.
Then your mind keeps on exploring,
the vast out reaches of space.
If it were within good taste,
I only have to wait a while
till other's come around,
then I will be found.
Off to explore
all my ideals.
The calculating mind is sharp,
every one has said their goodbyes.

*Nancy Susan Michael*

Then out that big, glass shining door
we go,
towards our destiny where ever it
may be,
forever more.
A touch of shine is not needed,
everything's been shined to suit,
even the best complainer.
It is great wisdom they are
embarking on a journey.
In my circle of friends I never knew
I had.
Gosh they are such loyal friends...
I can smile from ear to ear,
just knowing they will protect me
in the end.
Onward and upward the scale of
life we transcend.
Creeping through the vast reaches
of space.
In our minds we are fully ready,
to go where no man put asunder.
Do what you can do for today,
for tomorrow or the next may not
be
in our schedule.
Minuscule,
our seats fit snug around us.
Among the smiling faces surrounding
us,
our trip should be a swift one but
naught.

*Tinkering Around With Insanity*

With trial and error big clouds appear,
not a one sneaker or jeer.
The people are within full agreement,
congratulations and well wishes
have been sent.
Thusly it is heaven bound we be,
the heavenly galaxies we'd love
to see,
exploring them wouldn't be bad,
any reports we wouldn't have to cram.
It's a blessing our takeoff on ourselves
went well,
if it hadn't there would be sometime
between the next one.
For the pause that refreshes we stop
to take a small gasp.
Just floating around in all this beauty,
there must be the Lord out there.
So we pause to reflect,
upon our daily avenues of prayers,
in the darkest morning we've
ever seen,
with the stars still shining brightly.
Some good things just never
change,
it is always there just the way
you left it.
God forbid it ever change on us.
Each of us carries a mission
in our hearts to be
fulfilled,

*Nancy Susan Michael*

some things will never change,
the dark is still eerie and foreboding.
Our mission of good will will
be never ending.
We do this for our friends back home,
so we can feel free to roam.
Settled down is hard,
when space is cramped for some.
Space offers a challenge of
existing,
for we can't resist,
the ideal from liftoff to the
vast darkness of space,
is just like a rapid heart beat
eager to learn more,
just for the human race.
As we float in an inner existence,
we wonder where our nerve went.
Soon we settle down to an
existence of our own.
We're hoping we've survived the universe,
hope to see the Lord out there
in a new rebirth!

*Tinkering Around With Insanity*

# It's All Over

It's a cold fact of life
that when a bomb is dropped,
the mayhem that follows,
cannot be stopped.
The skin is pallor with fright.
What it must do for a child's
eyes,
really makes you stop and think.
Nothing will really perk you up,
not even someone's smile or
wink.
The air smells of day old smoke.
Smoke curls up from the ground.
This is no kind of hoax,
this kind of living will be found.
That living will not be at its best,
it shall be put to the test.
People around us dying of nerve
gas.
Death couldn't even let it pass.
It's ugly in a human being,
burnt skin hangs on the bones.
"My God," someone cried and
then couldn't.
Their eyeballs just don't focus.
There is nothing bogus about
this.

*Nancy Susan Michael*

In the west the sun set or did it?
Red sky at night sailor's delight
or is it?
Red sky all the time.
The bomb did it to show its
might.
The children's happy smiling
faces are no more.
There is no where for them to
play.
Up ahead you see a lonely
soldier,
just trying to get a bit bolder.
Scrambling, checking the ground
to see,
if there were any cigarette butts
unused or free.
If not, the soldier would use it
anyhow.
This man denounced the bomb
all right.
But it did no good.
It produced this ugly sight
for which he hoped those who
caused it,
could live with this ugly fright.
This was worst than any
Vietnam.
He sort of let out a cry.
He could just not stand by.
Up ahead he saw a band of
soldiers.

*Tinkering Around With Insanity*

Now which side were they on?
Guessing is just part of the fun.
The rest is understanding if they
happened to be on his side.
If not, this soldier will be
slapped, kicked, bitten, raped,
and
shot,
and left for dead.
You notice that time that goes by.
You notice that mostly none are
left.
But what happened to all the
women?
Where have most of them gone?
I shudder to think.
We certainly have our crosses to
burn,
while people stare.
This is what it's like in an
aftermath of a bomb.
All the prettiness of earth
will be gone.
In a split second it will be burnt.
It'll turn people into being surly
or curt.
The green trees will disappear.
The land will have no waves of
grain.
The purple mountain majesties
will be gone,
can't you see?

*Nancy Susan Michael*

The fruited plains
will be charred and ruined.
That poor lonely soldier,
who just doesn't care anymore,
tries to cry,
but then he can't.
He looks for his home
but cannot find it in the dust and
debris.
The soldier knows there is no
use looking.
For his home is no more.
The more you think about
dropping the bomb,
there is no turning back.
What you once had before,
which is politely put,
there are no jobs left to be had.
Our duties we cannot shirk.
A bomb ruins everything,
forever and ever.
So if at one time you had
something,
never will you know,
this poor soldier who
will probably never go home,
knows it all too well.
Up ahead he sees more soldiers,
sitting around a campfire.

*Tinkering Around With Insanity*

As he bravely approaches very softly,
he hopes that they have some food.
The soldiers are talking in the wrong dialect.
The soldier knew that when he got to them,
that he wouldn't survive.
He carried a small pocket bible, opened to Genesis.
The soldier spoke...
"In the Beginning..."
read the soldier.
In front of him appeared a white cross from out of nowhere.
Then suddenly the soldier heard shots from out of nowhere.
He fell to the ground bent over in despair.
"Read" the Lord whispered him,
"I shall not want..."
The Lord ordered him to crawl out of his body towards the white cross.
The Lord appeared above the cross ready to receive the soldier.
The Lord raised the soldier from the ground up to his waiting arms.

*Nancy Susan Michael*

The soldier, laying in the Lords arms,
floated upward with the Lord.
With the soldier repeating...
"Ashes to ashes,"
"Dust to dust,"
"The Lord is my Sheppard,"
"I shall never want...!"
"The bomb and me,"
"I'll never again of it get the brunt..."
"For I'm finally one with the Lord,
This is my home now,
I'll finally be set free!"

## Approving the New Year

As I approach the New Year,
I am wise to the facts,
that in order to make love last,
you can't buy it off the store rack.
Love is something to be cultivated,
that you first want to be taken in.
With a kiss it must be kept moist.
When the weight of the world is upon us,
the only fuss should be over us.
In order to make this last,
you add a dash of caring.
A pinch of sighing.
Mixing it together by being close.
At New Year's make a toast,
may your lips seal what you boast.
It is forever written that,
there is no given room for slack,
is a hot relationship filled with love.
You must first be caring,
taking things slow and easy,
to avoid any of nature's teasing.
If it is possible to love too much,
then so what if we are guilty?
It is nobodies business,
if your lips meet or not.
Being together means everything,
if it is really to work.
Fan the flames a bit higher,
acting like a live wire.

*Nancy Susan Michael*

Your lips meet together despite,
it other's think it is right.
It has taken over the night,
love has taken over the years,
to make the closeness seen right.
If it were within my power,
if it were within my last right,
I'd protect you from any known scrutiny.
Within what powers in me I have,
I'd pull you close and let love explode.
I'd sit by a warm fireside.
My arms around you tighten their grip.
I'd quickly pick you out among all
the rest.
I'd never rate you second best.
Your are top's in what you do,
all I know is how well you do it.
I can feel your love and passion,
miles and miles away.
With me it shall always stay,
between the two of us where it belongs.
In my heart I have a song,
us to we want to sing a long.
For your love does make life more
bearable,
there is nothing to compare to our love!
Love is the start of an adventure,
in which only two can share.
It is always found in the cards,
a love as strong as ours.

*Tinkering Around With Insanity*

You don't want to hop around,
when together our flames ignite into passion.
A strong beginning with love,
giving love day after day.
Keeping in time with each other's cryptic ideas.
The shape of our love will always be great.
Another twenty-five years in the making,
will teach us to be like old pros.
It gives you that warm, wonderful feeling,
that only the two of us can produce.
It gives you that all over feeling,
that can evaporate into your very soul.
Our love is always motivated,
to cleanse our very soul.
Our love is never underrated,
it is always motivated.
My how time does fly.
It seems like time goes by so quickly,
when we're together.
May our love prosper and grow.
Just to show us it is ours.
For us it will always be.
It is the love that awaits us.
It is a rhapsody in the key of 'G' minor,
our love couldn't be anything
but finer!

*Nancy Susan Michael*

# Awaken Your Senses

I'd like to awaken your senses,
by being all of your
wildest desires.
Whatever you happen to dream of,
I'd like to be that person and
really do it with style.
I'd try to please you in any
way I could.
I'd change your whole constitution
if only I would.
I'd do it just to your specifications,
I'd never walk around any notions
you might have of being
less than perfect.
You are perfect to me in my eyes,
and I wish I could give you vitality.
I'd give you everything that
would change you completely,
into just the person you want
to be.
We are the exact opposites but
I believe we love each other
dearly,
it will be so till the end of
our time,
we both have our pride.
To let no one stand in the way,

*Tinkering Around With Insanity*

I hope each day and pray,
as each chance we get to be together.
Our love in our life will have a purpose to serve!

*Nancy Susan Michael*

# A Song In Your Heart

Always wear a song in your heart,
for we are meant never to part.
Even though the going gets rough,
it's when everyone starts getting tough.
And let nothing better then,
for there is a big message to send.
Since you are meant to be together,
we two will create quite a stir.
In all that is said and done,
why remove all the fun?
That can be had from a loving relationship,
that sends you on a real trip.
And puts a stride in your step,
that gives you lot's of pep.
And puts a smile on your face,
that wrinkle lines cannot erase.
This is what two people in love can bring,
joy to their hearts when they sing.
Songs of joy and caring,
love is over powering and daring.
It is not just a passing fancy,
that leave's you dancing.
There is something floating in the air,
which means you must show each other you care.
For love is written all over our faces,
and can be found in the most unlikely places!

## Twist of Luck

It had to be a twist of luck we met,
you see,
and you took the lead.
In a dance I'll always remember,
I can't remember if it was in September.
But I sunk into your arms,
that didn't do any harm.
It felt so good and I fell for all your
charms,
I wish I met you sooner, darn.
Since that first dance,
you've put me in a trance.
You lifted my spirits up high,
for you anything I'd try.
You got me to see,
how much you mean to me.
I never know just what is in store,
for you make me soar.
Everytime I see you come by,
it makes me want to reach for the sky.
In almost anything I do dear,
without shedding a tear.
It is for you and only you,
that I'll be true.
What all you do for me dear,
you take away all my fear.
And you replace it with love unlike
no other darling,
a romance with us starring.

*Nancy Susan Michael*

# What You Mean to Me

What you mean to me is everything,
you make it so my voice can sing.
When I down and out,
you make me hold up my head and shout.
For you I'd do just about anything,
even go soaring out on a bird's wing.
I have to wait to catch my flight,
oh, must that be a sight.
You make my future a whole lot brighter,
when you kiss me and squeeze me tighter.
I don't want to out up a fuss,
but to please you is a must.
But I hope that someday I'll please you,
and in hope you'll see me too.
I hold onto your love with all my might,
at sometimes I may look a fright.
I feel like something's not quite right,
your love is something in which I delight.
But haven't you felt that way before,
when I told you what was in store.
Haven't you ever felt that way before,
before I become a real bore
when things get down and out,
I just want to stand and shout.
Leaving me would not be right,
for it makes our love tight.
I will love you more and more,
it is you that I adore.
As we sit and stare and each other,

*Tinkering Around With Insanity*

I pray to God as it were.
To keep each other's love in check,
as slowly through life I trek.
I only want to please him more,
forever and ever
my husband is the one I really adore.

*Nancy Susan Michael*

# The Power of Forgiveness

The power of forgiveness
is strong,
it is like the sunrise in the morning.
A forgiveness happens with
a smile, that grows wider and wider.
It can create a bond,
between two people who are fond.
Of each other so great,
no one can permiate.
There is no mistake,
that two in love is
a high rating.
The existence of a bond
that's real,
that no one can mistake.
In the richness only,
one can partake.
Make no mistake about it,
love is great form
where I sit.
It takes a lot of give,
and as long as I live.
All that I can do for you,
before the day is true
I'll try to please you too.
With all kinds of delight,
with things that are
out-of-sight.

*Tinkering Around With Insanity*

Such are the feelings only
two can share,
approach only if you dare.
To share and know
we care.
We certainly have had our share,
of ups and downs with
room-to-spare.
For each and every woe, our love will not go.
By the wayside ever throughout,
our love will last throughout
whatever bout'.
Since we can truly say,
no matter who tries to
break us up,
on that we have already
jumped.
A word to the wise,
don't even try!

*Nancy Susan Michael*

# In my Power

If it were in my power,
I would start.
With changing the world,
in which we live.
I'd erase the ugliness.
Remove all the ridicule.
I put you on the thrown dear.
Make sure to right every wrong.
I'd see to it,
that each and every person,
had its own feelings.
Surrounded with love,
and criticism gone.
Least it show up,
be banished form the world.
Each and every day,
would be a bright new experience.
For each and every person,
upon the face of the earth.
People love smiles,
and also caring faces.
Name dropping would disappear,
and life and reality.
Would be a much better place to be.
From when out of every mouth,
there came a wrong,
let us place it,
where it belongs.

*Tinkering Around With Insanity*

It does not need
a place in society,
to be socially downcast,
it is not reality.
I for one I agree instead of
laughing at one,
turn it around,
and laugh at yourself.
It causes unbelievable pain.
which most can't hide.
You shake it down to size.
You shake it down to size,
yet it shows up again.
It's hard to deal with,
life gets tedious.
You cant do anything,
but suffer too much.
If I had my way,
this world will be a better place.
Once people realize,
what they can do,
to help their own plight.
Understanding and love,
goes a much longer ways.
I say without trepidation,
marvelous things come.
To he who practices the art
of love and not downsizing.
No matter what race,
color or creed,
the idea is still the same.

*Nancy Susan Michael*

Instead of spreading hatred,
that eats away the soul.
It makes a better day.
for a friendly smile.
Or possibly a hi.
The cure is love,
instead of labeling.
Listen to what I say,
for me and all others.
That to teach a lesson,
should be tempered with love,
not hate.
Hate is the most ugly thing,
in life you're missing,
a beautiful happening.
when applying love,
not hate!

*Tinkering Around With Insanity*

# Death by Consciousness

Death by consciousness is a dive out of
reality into the dark,
for the subconscious has to dive to part.
Put the two together and you have
death of the soul,
which on the brain takes its toll.
The brain just ceases to be,
but just in case any life form belongs to me.
It is merely a passing phase to you,
for you and your brain are not through.
And as it pulsates and jerks one more time,
it gives a little jerk and off it signs.
Into a void of darkness—by choice,
your imagination is lifted up by a hoist.
The hoist is a chemical which creates dreams,
and this particular phase does not scheme.
It completely relaxes you as you make,
as your mind is in a dream phase take,
pictures of the dark and tell me what you thing,
do not let your heart be discouraged
and sink.
The reality is the darkness and what
we make of it,
or simply put what we believe it to be
as you see fit.
Whatever your beliefs will carry you through.
For now is the time to access those beliefs
and it's long overdue,
whatever your beliefs will see you through.

*Nancy Susan Michael*

For now is the time to access those
beliefs and pay your dues
All your life it has been just tailor made for you,
so you an hold to your feelings
that seem to be true,
So it is all in how you believe each of you
on how death affects only a few.

## On a Journey of Love

On a journey of love, in our life one must travel,
while great mysteries and love a story can unravel.
it is really amazing what life can hold,
for two people in love may be bold.
It is a one-of-a-kind story ever said,
to adorn the pages of a book to be read.
Who can only read the best, enough said.
The best of you and me is yet to be,
no matter who puts us down, just wait and see.
In this world the best cure is love,
but so is the two people who
fit together like a kid glove.
Two people with a love like ours is hard to find,
knowing love is the test that blinds.
Even the best relationships experience rough waters,
and in all that you do,
it never hurts to improve.
And then there's you and me,
a relationship that I think is just fine.
We have the meaning of love,
that can withstand the test of time.

*Nancy Susan Michael*

# Forever Lost in Love

There are some couples who will be forever
lost in love,
and it is most noticeable that one of
those is us.
Our love is sent from heaven above,
it makes the wind blow and
the leaves rustle.
It is the strength behind many
great earthquakes,
why I believe our love is strong enough
never to forsake.
It is as strong as the tide that whips
upon the shore,
it is different in intensity as never to
be a bore.
It is strong enough to make the planets rotate
around the sun,
as such our love gravitates to us strongly proved
to be fun.
It is that glow that is put
on our faces,
that helps light the way when we
visit new places.
It gives us hopes and dreams
for the future,
such as a doctor sewing trouble up
with a suture.
It gives us hope when our lives feel down,
it maps out a plan in life to keep us
safe and sound.

## Tinkering Around With Insanity

it helps to be forever lost in
love so bad,
that you never call each
other a cad.
It is from great heights
where eagles soar,
for without it we'd all be bores.
And just suppose it was strong enough to dam
up a river,
or calming enough not to set our nerves
in a dither.
how about clearing enough to calm the worst
storms in life,
but wet enough to give our life rain
from which our love can derive.
A substance which helps it grow and grow,
through which many of life's force through
us can show,
Love is a builder of a stubborn strength
and lasting entity,
for it helps you make an impact with any
type of density.
Love is behind the stars
that shine brightly,
shining enough to give us all
kinds of insight.
I guess in closing our love was just
meant to be,
strong, enduring, ever-lasting
in this eternity!

*Nancy Susan Michael*

## A Fantasy Ride

Let us take a fantasy ride together,
and celebrate what we
have is special.
As a ferris wheel goes up and down,
so can life's many problems cause
us lot's of woes to be found.
But somehow our marriage has withstood
the test of time.,
just like clockwork for each other
we pine.
Life is like a train going around
the park,
life can give you your share of
headaches.
That's what makes the world go round
and give you a jump start,
life can be like a river boat sailing
down the river,
it is not always calm sailing and rough
waters can set you in a dither.
Just like your haunted mansions you see,
that the ghosts in your life can
cause your problems that you can feel.
Take a game of chance it is that way
with life,
if you take your chances you
may have strife,
and there may be problems which
we won't like.

*Tinkering Around With Insanity*

I think we go together like bread and butter,
you are the one that sets my heart
a flutter,
and sends orgasmic pleasure
throughout my body,
you drive me just a little 'dottie.'
To me you are just like honey,
for me you make a rainy day sunny.
You feel so good to lay next to,
and your kisses just set me free.
I just want you to know how
good you are for me,
just for the whole world to see.
You give me strength and courage
to go on,
for you put in my life
all the fun.
It is you that I live for,
you're the only man that I adore.
I have chosen you for my one and only,
you make me feel pretty not homely.
So it goes without saying that,
you are the best man to be my husband
and that is a fact!

*Nancy Susan Michael*

# A Parkinson's Love

A Parkinson's love can be for the finer
things in life for,
after all do they deserve it
more.
What kind of good things in life could
this be?
A want of food, clothes, shelter, and
nothing's free.
It is hard for these people to
move about,
especially when it stalls them or they
'can't chill out.'
It is our love we have for each other
a special kind,
it was sheer luck that we met
at that time.
Of course as each Parkinson's patient knows
a marriage is rough with this,
to help it last forever takes
a big wish.
it takes a lot of work I admit,
also a lot of brawn and wit.
A love that stands out to all the rest
can put things to the test.
Of course getting back to other things
what Parkinson's people
need is a lot of love,
plus understanding from society
thereof.

*Tinkering Around With Insanity*

And a cure to be found soon.
For only darkness around every corner
the PD patient looms.
They need love, encouragement, smiling faces,
and in bad need of a cure,
but sometimes only leads to expenses
and a lure.
Of stories of promises that don't hold water
you just about need to win
the lotto.
The medical field puts up hopes and
promises,
but the problems and causes from
promises damages.
The very heart and soul of the patient,
who's heart is cut and his soul bent.
I feel that brain surgery is
not the cure,
for the outcome of most has proven
not to be sure.
You never feel quite right afterwards,
and for the most part you run
the a close third.
So in life the Parkinson's patient,
one who counts most with
me is my spouse.
No matter what other's think I
think that's what counts!
Being loved by such a lovely man as he,
brings out the best in me.
He has a big say in my life,
and I'm proud to be his wife.

*Nancy Susan Michael*

Out of all the possible cures on time
that is best spent,
is to your husband or wife how
the time went...
For being with him and being
his wife,
I consider it to be a great life.
The little things in life are the
best I find,
for his kisses hold promise and
are sweeter than wine.
And that is my cure I have found,
to be the most outstanding
around!

*Tinkering Around With Insanity*

# Monsters and Demons

Monsters and demons come in all sizes,
the best one's come from the word
of the wise.
When we start to see demons it's a new
kind of art.
It is time to take stock,
on what we're all about.
For these things are a creation,
which deserve a highly shared rating,
They are not just from the
earth or moon,
they are from the drinks we inject, after we croon.
We see those little devils only in June,
and gosh all over the place they
seem to bloom.
That's when it really gets
you into trouble,
when you keep on insisting they exist,
it makes you wonder.
You sit and mutter they exist
and make more blunders,
the more you drink the more they start,
they stand up and laugh at
you and dare.
Why are you chosen one for
their fan-faire?
We will pick at you and bug you too,'
you drank too many drinks and a lot of
money you blew.

## Nancy Susan Michael

So you did this the night before,
you drank and drank so you have a
treat in store.
It is all the fault of the 'Lost Lenore.'
For this is a responsibility you bore.
The first one you saw was on the counter, '
"Hail to the Chief," you wanted a gun and
gunpowder.
For they were approaching with full force,
they were so ugly neither one of them could
I could carry a torch.
Who'd want to romance one of them anyhow,
for anything like them I'd have the whole
earthy to scour.
It was after this I threw up my
beer and pretzels,
they cloned all over the place when I tried
to meddle.
I wanted to share my peanuts and pretzels,
just so they wouldn't in my armpits and
stomach nestle.
I stood up and drew in a deep breath,
then I saw the mother of them all, what
an ugly ol' wretch!',
and tried to blow them to kingdom come
all over the place,
for my band with the pretzels they
did race.
It was those weird little antenna's they
had,
only they used them like pogo sticks on the
bottom of their feet how sad!

## Tinkering Around With Insanity

It's not to my wanderings eyes did not appear,
for I was becoming unglued as a space
ship was heading up the rear.
I laughed and laughed so hard it hurt,
for they tried spitting me in spurts.
Between the spitting and the pogo sticks,
looking at them I almost with my cigarette
burnt my nose down to the wick.
So before I set the bar on fire,
I went through my mind
with complete desire.
To find out what got me in this
shape,
it must have been that man wearing
that red cape.
No it does matter to me,
I think it was in that green drink
she said 'wait and see.'
So I finally took stock of what
was going on,
I figured out fast I had to go
to the John.
So I got up and walked away,
into a deep dark pit I fell and I
started to pray.
Then a sad lesson to learn, that
dark pit was I had passed out,
and wound up in a Dt center with
people who have a alcohol bouts.
So may God our merry ol' souls,
being a drunk is a strange roll.
For whether you're in a center or not,

*Nancy Susan Michael*

I'm afraid those little green men will
stay with you,
no matter what in lot your life.
For if you remember before you passed out,
you stuffed a few in your pocket,
just so you could play a turnabout!

*Tinkering Around With Insanity*

# The Last Train

I was always there in life,
to always catch the last train.
To put it mildly, I was always that way,
till there was you.
You are my guiding light.
Forever you are my soul and inspiration.
You lift me up to the sky.
Around you I don't feel timid.
I feel like I can conquer the world.
I don't feel as if I've been stepped on.
The weight of the world is not a ton.
With you I know I can,
forever see a way that's righteous.
Just fitting and proper for me.
Who is this miraculous person I ask.
It is the only one I can look up to.
I see my way clearly before me.
He follows the same path too.
He sends my spirits soaring,
with the greatest feelings of love.
Given to none other than,
me and the response is mutual.
For me it is like,
a breath of spring air.
A lily of the valley,
that will keep us both happy.
Our spirits have shown the test of time.
The fact that we will never fear.

*Nancy Susan Michael*

We won't even shed a tear.
As we fondly remember dear.
During our moments of triumph.
Through the good and the bad.
It's just like Swan Lake.
Across the lake.
All different colors, sizes and shapes,
the meaning they give is peace.
You have shown me love and a peace in
my life unlike no other.
We have made it through the test of
time.
This is just another test we are going
through.
It is one in which we shall make it.
No matter what is put forth to us.
We all have axes to grind,
or bridges to cross.
But we seem to make it easier with each
other.
No matter what we must look the other
way.
Hang in there for old times sake.
Let no others walk above us.
What we have is too special to break the
mold.
It is a wise man who once said,
'never give up.'
If you give up totally then you have
truly lost.
If you hang in there and fight for what
you believe in.

*Tinkering Around With Insanity*

Then it is you I must believe in.
You hold the key to my happiness.
You are my Christmas Package all
wrapped into one.
We can let elements cause trouble
between us.
For I feel our love is too great for that to
happen.
It is up to us dear and us alone.
To let other's know the love we've shown
each other
is for ourselves alone.
Let waves of discord not tear us apart.
But give us a new lease on life, one with
a head start!

*Nancy Susan Michael*

# Way Back When

Many of us sit and count the days,
Till we are older.
But let us not forget that when
We get older, we must get bolder.
We fight furiously for the day,
When we sit and say,
We want to get older,
But why must we pay?
We have our good days and bad,
Some better than others,
So why sit and worry about,
Another bout with age...
We want to age gracefully,
God know that's hard to do
So if we can't be true to ourselves,
To whom can we be true blue?
Only to ourselves when we answer to who?

*Tinkering Around With Insanity*

# A Winged Flight

A winged flight is in the offing,
For each and everyone of us.
Right now if it fit it could
Give us quite the rush.
Unforeseen unlike before,
It holds in store.
For us to go through that door.
Have you made your reservation?
You must have patience.
For you've had all your life,
To make up your mind how,
You see fit to travel.
On one of those winged flights.
It will stop right beside us,
You will hop on aboard.
Take your seat up front,
Grasp the situation at hand.
Well it looks like full speed ahead.
As the captain wanders out of the cockpit,
You feel free to introduce yourself.
the stewardess walks out,
Just as pretty as can be.
You'd really like to know her now.
Her face you could really adore.
As you settle back in your seat,
You happen to notice something.
As you look around this particular flight,

*Nancy Susan Michael*

You notice you are the only one on the airplane.
You can't right now,
But you will completely soon,
You reach
Just to figure out if you're there.
When you pinched yourself it hurt.
You dropped your cigarette and almost got burnt.
Then you ordered a can of beer,
Then you figured out you had nothing to fear.
It also came with pretzels and nuts.
Oh their stuff everyone will strut.
Wait until I call home.
To tell them about this flight.
Here I sit and look out this window,
Where am I going?
When did I make this flight?
Your suspicions won't light.
It was your plight.
So you decided to stay aboard.
Without a quibble you look out the window.
The airplane roared up its engines.
He felt the plane release its brake.
The takeoff was great.
Fasten your safety belt.

## Tinkering Around With Insanity

The Captain yelled,
"This will be a trip you'll never forget."
As your plane ascends,
The air gets thinner,
You feel as though you're a winner!
As the plane straightens out,
You settle down for another bout.
As you look out the window.
You can see some of the different things.
You see your first stop sign.
As you look about the plane.
You thought you saw Father Time.
You glared at him in vain.
He yelled at you saying,
It is now time to go upward.
As if on the flight of a bird.
You wave back to Father Time.
To you he was very kind.
Then the plane leaves him,
To take another turn.
What you see puts you in awe.
What you see next,
You just want to bawl.
For a fact you don't know what's next.
What you saw next,
Rated you with the best,
Were all your dead friends,
Their houses with them in them

Laughing and carrying on.
They had been gone for many years.
You decided then you had died,
Your destiny was left up to the Lord.
To strike a happy accord,
You decided you were on your way to heaven.
The plane made a sudden stop.
"This is where you got off,"
the Captain announced.
So off you go onto the red carpet,
There was nothing else around.
You were supposedly on cloud bank number 9,
The first stage in heaven.
Down the Red Carpet lane you went,
Messages were sent.
You approached,
The Pearly gates of Heaven,
Of which you cried out for joy.
Let me in dear Lord to be with you,
I know I'm in the right place now,
For I'm nobodies fool !
Thank you Lord for the fantasy!!

## My Only One

If there was my only one,
It would have to be you.
There is no other one who thrills me,
Quite like you do.
You are heaven's excitement,
that creates a stir in me.
You set my sights skyward.
Enveloping me in love like no other.
Ours will never be a dying ember.
I know our love to be special,
So we are exact opposites.
For me it is the most real thing,
You being my only reality.
Who to think us two would have met,
Only if the stars encouraged it!

*Nancy Susan Michael*

# In A Way

In the way life can be strange
Or it can be hum-drum and plain.
Within reasonable limits of sanity,
Life is ours to experiment with
Commonly called vanity.
It has with it a range
Of emotions,
Of which can be tons and tons.
In a way it is the best,
To sort them out from
All the rest,
Stock pile them for later use,
Keeping them from verbal
Also physical abuse.
To do so with what we may,
Even though many don't see it.

## Oh I Pray

I bequeath to you my love
ever lasting so much more.
Before I'd close any door
my heart I do care for.
We do have something beautiful,
unlike all the riches of the earth.
It's just like the waves of the wild
pounding surf,
our love for each other not aloof,
but down to earth
enough to make others look.
What you see are two people
who believe
what is their legacy
in this world to be?
Full of prying eyes,
automatic suggestions
asking no questions.
Loving each other,
never to ever close any doors,
on anything so warn and tender,
as what we have forever,
in that light of love and romance,
you and I steal the show!

*Nancy Susan Michael*

# Beauty In The Beholder

There is beauty every where we
see it,
We can look for It anywhere,
Beauty can be viewed in
Many different ways.
It should show beauty right then
and there.
Our personalities have beauty in
them,
They can shine or bring us down,
Whether you wear a smile
Or a frown.
When in life we see beauty
everywhere,
On a child's face at Christmas time.
There is beauty in that Christmas
tree,
Which the decorations and tree
lights it bore.
that Christmas day when Jesus
Was born,
We sit and reflect what the day
really means,
We can share in a child's delight as
to what this day can bring.
It is the star upon the tree that
sparkles so bright,
The wreath on the door that sets
things off right,

*Tinkering Around With Insanity*

The aroma of cooking from the
kitchens,
Says Christmas is in the air and
the
Celebration begins.
It is Yuletide carolers,
And children frolic
Having a good time romping
In the snow.
So we see the beauty,
In the day Christ was born,
As children wake to a Christmas born
in the likeness of Jesus.
Why we don't have to look too far
to find beauty,
For it's in everyone we look at and
see all around,
for beauty is truly in the eye of the beholder!

*Nancy Susan Michael*

# Best In Life

What I seem to think are the best
things in life,
may differ with another's point of view.
My philosophy maybe all wrong or my
general idea of 'what to do'.
It doesn't coincide with the given,
so I can't hand out any dividends.
I'm not perfect in everyone's eyes,
Lord knows I never professed to try.
If it were within my established bounds,
I'm just like a ticking clock, 'all wound'.
In this imperfect world I find,
I must learn to take things in stride.
Don't know how I'll complete that feat,
unless I learn how to coincide.
Sometimes take a back seat.
In this life we can not always be an
Einstein,
or be a wholesale Jean seller like
Calvin Klein...
Either the can may be.
We are established here on earth,
as far as the eye can see,
not to just do our thing,
but to accept our lot in life,
and to see just what it brings.
All the well trotted path in life you
may get a few flat tires.
But never fear there is always that bicycle

*Tinkering Around With Insanity*

pump,
that when used carefully,
will carry you over all the bumps.
In this life Lord knows,
there happen to be a lot of them,
why sometimes it frightens you so.
You hate to open the door.
It's like a seed planted in the ground.
Water it and watch it grow.
Without the water,
it will eventually take its toll.
The seed won't grow at all.
In this life we must watch,
what we say and do.
It can sometimes harm creativity in a few
that do.
We were all not broken from the same
mold,
for if that were true, unkind words would
never be spoken.
Since we don't live in such a perfect world,
it is up to us to stick to our pride.
Not to put away for tomorrow,
what we don't want to hide.
Life is however which way you can make a
difference.
Whatever way we look at life is solely
up to you.
You will reveal everything in your actions,
what you say and do!

*Nancy Susan Michael*

# Whispers of Roses

If roses could only talk,
what would they say?
In this life they could if only you
pray.
They would say something most fitting,
it's Christmas time, proper for romance
knitting.
It's a cup of hot chocolate by the fireside.
It's the yuletide and eggnog on Christmas
day.
The stockings all hung by the chimney with care.
The snowflakes wafting in through an open door.
The fireside crackling with excitement.
The poinsettia's all laid out against the
spiral staircase.
Just a hint of the morning sun strikes
through a pane of glass.
The cold wind whispers around the corners
of the house.
Angels seem to be dancing on a fire light.
A bird chirps on its winged flight
through the chilled air.
Ol' Saint Nick eating his cookies and milk.
Santa with those guilty looking eyes.
Going for a sleigh ride out in the
cool, crisp air.
The children bounding down the stairs on
a chilly Christmas morning.

*Tinkering Around With Insanity*

Just to see what Santa
brought.
Eager to unwrap presents galore,
just to see what they have in store.
Roses delivered again to the front door,
oh what stories they can tell.
Children running back and forth.
Whispering how to plan the day.
Carolers knocking at the door.
Bringing Yuletide Christmas cheer.
The children learning what Christmas means.
Waiting to take their new sleighs outside.
Bright red mittens and scarves.
The house merely jumping with excitement.
The beautifully wrapped packages,
out under the tree.
All different, tin foil, ribbons and
the size of the packages.
Children romping about singing Christmas songs.
Eagerly getting on with the business of Christmas.
Neighbors stopping by for a friendly
chat.
A look outside the door at a vast
countryside.
The family dog barking wildly at the
chilled air outside.
Spacing yourself between intervals of
excitement.
Watching the electric go round and round
under the tree.
The star on top twinkles each time the
trains shakes the tree.

*Nancy Susan Michael*

A gift to the wife in the name of love.
Light shining through the roses,
as if they could talk.
In the name of God have a Merry Christmas.
We'll meet you Christmas morning in
church to pray!

## Spare the Lonely

Despite the reality of being,
that has crept into our very soul,
it breathed upon its victims,
that without a bottle of Rum,
that will take care of some.
Some of whom always seem to be lonely.
It is without conviction,
as we actually just a sittin',
sittin' at the corner of the walkway.
Must we always have to pay,
pay for our stingy ways.
It is the mean bare facts of life,
that it is quite a sight,
when you see one who drinks,
everything but the kitchen sink.
This person does it within a wink,
just to keep within the pink.
He is on a discovery brink.
What is it like when you take
too many drinks,
this person can't even think.
As you slowly sip, sip, sip,
particles of your life you rip, rip, rip.
When suddenly you feel as tho'
you've been on a trip.
Out where no man has gone before.
We seem to take stock in
what we have in store.

*Nancy Susan Michael*

For we learn real fast the score.
This is when our minds,
look through a drunken haze to find,
our salvation is on the line.
That is when we hope to find,
what it takes from a drunken stupor
to unwind.
Why must we drink to find,
to find all the wrong company,
but never the fight company,
but turns out to be half way.
People who drink are a sorry lot,
who can't quite fit into life's plot.
It's over life's discord when struck,
into the heart's of many it plucks.
They start getting ancy,
when the drinks start getting fancy,
they soon discover no matter
what, life goes on.
Take away the bottle removes all the fun,
when you remove the bottles of Rum.
When life gets rough you seek
out the Lord,
with His help on ahead you forge.
Without the help of this deity you
can't do a thing,
seek Him out to se what joys he brings.
So when it gets you down spunky,
we shouldn't drink till we get chunky.

*Tinkering Around With Insanity*

Then throw up all over our nice, dry streets,
you definitely march to a different drum's beat,
because you can't take the heat.
Instead you take a loss in your life,
you should look for what
is right,
you're out walking the streets instead.
Thinking about what might have been.
Looking back doesn't help,
you've got to take that first step.
Over broken pieces of your life.
All because you sat there and wept,
over broken pieces of your life.
So despite all the odds,
some of us don't feel quite so dumb,
when thinking about what might have been.
You have to pick up the pieces
and start over.
Into life head first you dove,
like a boat anchored in a cove.
You are ready to set sail once again,
a timely message you have sent.
In this case you haven't lost,
when you finally discover who's boss,
a trip to your local church to pray,
will not be for a loss!

*Nancy Susan Michael*

# Stronger Than Ever

A passion ignites between us,
igniting a fire a must.
A love deep in thought,
Father Time in seconds bought.
Eagerness to be together.
Through any endeavor.
A sparkle of love in the eye,
you recently ask yourself why.
Not ever to be judged.
From each other needn't budge.
Turning it into a love affair.
Going where hearts have not gone before.
Enjoying every minute of it.
Wrapped up in each other's arms.
Their hearts beating as one.
Searching each other eye's.
All in the name of love.
With love it can't be rough.
If you've got the right stuff.
A chemistry unlike no other.
It's no trouble to be there.
You both are so thankful.
For time well spent.
It is just like being in heaven,
our love we both enjoy!

## Looking For A Pardon

Looking for a pardon if you can.
Possibly find one left around,
a prayer if you may,
you can always be found
having your say.
Looking for it may or may not
make your day.
In your mind I won't lose track,
in your erroneous ideas I won't bask.
Your own mind has to be emptied,
many ideas over which I've wept.
It's not something to file back
in your mind.
If you're looking in some unusual place,
where it just won't be a waste.
Start looking into the back of your mind,
restitution I can't find.
If it is before the Lord you knelt,
perhaps your mind works like
a conveyor belt.
That is why your ideas went from
front to back,
of your mind it was sent.
Around and around it went somewhere,
just enough to make it a threat or scare.
Just enough to lose your pardon from God.
It isn't something you've won,
for on your mind it weighs a ton,
you need some light perhaps the sun.

*Nancy Susan Michael*

For two people who want their pardon,
to make it all better.
It is best to vent,
your feelings out loud.
Raise your voice in unison.
Lord, I want to be heard,
I threw you this lonely surge.
Do not ever purge,
on the idea of getting to know God.
Simply savor the hours and minutes,
then don't be so timid,
about asking for a handout.
Do not carry on your face a pout,
between you and God ask not.
You get time when you ask at the right time.
Do not wear a face mask,
to hide all the efforts you've made.
Through the muddy waters you wade.
All for this you wouldn't trade,
without the knowledge of God you're insane.
To think about traveling to
greater heights through eternity.
A concept only which your mind can conceive.
When God says no he doesn't want you,
look around at what you must do.
To find treasure of God
within you,
you mustn't,
just so you wouldn't look like a fool.
Keeping God's love is the Golden Rule,
keeping the faith that we won ourselves.
Accepting God's faith into the Hall of Fame.

*Tinkering Around With Insanity*

It is your own special way.
For your own love of God will last.
Time can go by too fast.
God's love will keep you from saying
HI.
Before the days end,
that we welcome God with all our hearts and might,
may be right anything that's wrong in spite!

Nancy Susan Michael

# Hearts of Many

We figure prominently in the hearts of many.
All around this world of ours,
Just to see if I can still
Put out any kind of poetry.
I thank the Lord above if this is
A given gift,
Though the archives of my mind I sift,
My memory banks for a verse or poem
That gives me a lift.
If it weren't for a man made machine,
I may have never been able to rhyme,
Much less tell a story with it,
So that makes me a poet author with
A bit of wit...
I say just a bit of wit,
Because I find it surprising what
I have up there,
For I can tell a story of woe,
Or even one that scares.
I didn't expect to be a winner,
But win at life if one can,
Did I ever surprise them mom,
If a poet's place in this world
I did land...
Don't know how I did it,
I still haven't come down off cloud nine,
But if I can make people laugh and
Make them cry too,

*Tinkering Around With Insanity*

Also helps to chase away the blues...
That's y poetry and what it's about,
It's been great fun just trying,
I needed a burst to my life I just got
The trophy cup and medallion...
What a great feat for little ol' me.
I'm back to Susan Lucci again,
I just love her attitude...
It depicts mine in a nutshell,
Before I cause my head to swell.
If a joke is a joke and I can take it...
A winning attitude is even better,
For now I can hold my head up high,
And say for once in life I tried...
So what a high I did get...
I wish I could have been there better yet...
I was there in my dreams,
Just winding down planning my next scheme.
What shall I attribute all this to?
Just fun, talent(?), and a skeptical old Fool!

*Nancy Susan Michael*

# Within My Grasp

If it were within my grasp,
I would make a covenant with God.
It would create within me a bond,
of which it could be found,
encirculating me with love.
Then I would do all I could,
to make sure that I
could be found,
trying to do the right thing.
If at first I don't succeed,
I'll try and do some type
of good deed.
In order to seal my part with God,
I have this time or duration,
it might cost me in prescription.
In the long run it was worth it.
It goes without saying that...
the burden is within your grasp.
To help you perform and task.
If you don't do it all in one
whack.
It is a most enterprising
thing to do,
to make sure you aren't a fool.
When I reach a certain point,
within all my cares and woes.
My wild oats I've sewn.

## *Tinkering Around With Insanity*

My goodwill for the day is blown,
if it is within the realm of
being realistic,
you certainly don't need a mystic.
You don't lead the perfect life,
when things seem to get a bit trifle.
Your feather's are all ruffled,
your disposition is a might gruff.
The wrong ride of the bed is not your forte,
when things just don't seem
to be right.
When they seem to get you quickly,
they just aren't apple pie and silk,
when things get you down.
The concept is too hard to grasp,
pick up the bible and study about God.
He can handle life's many problems,
he does it really easily with a golden rod!

*Nancy Susan Michael*

# A Way Of Meaning

A way of meaning,
What do you want?
For starters do you want
a head start in life?
Getting out on the
right side of bed would help.
The wrong side of bed
gives us two left feet.
Oh, what you wouldn't give,
To have that quick pick-me-upper!
To help you relieve,
like time goes together.
An hourglass for you,
A real meaning is,
we can reach for the sky forever.
If you dare,
it needn't be explained.
Off a mistake,
yet you partake,
in every idea you make.
You aim to please,
in all that you do.
I if I can't be myself.
then who can I be?
When your luck runs out,
everyone has to part,
that you can market
when things go astray.

## Tinkering Around With Insanity

Don't let things get so bad,
why are you so sad?
When your efforts are futile,
I know you'll do it in style.
Just to be the best there is,
puts us all sometimes in a
deep well.
Though we don't want,
to go there,
isn't it just as fair?
That you even the score,
by spouting off some more.
Is this the way of meaning,
that your different emotions,
can really get us down?
When we can usually be found,
Uttering utterances that are unfounded.
All your thoughts are not ungrounded
by superficial fears.
Terrified of your own tears,
that you go through this.
When imagination is not a given,
By the light we are guided,
To have our own say.
To tower over the mundane,
an excuse is intolerable.
Some I ideas will be dissolvable,
if you listen to,
the benefit of experience.
The older people shine,
a way of meaning,
without it being demeaning.

*Nancy Susan Michael*

Their ideas are eccentric we think,
but most of them are relics.
Poorly formed ideas can change
to stand on their own.
The oldster makes it grand,
on its own idea to stand,
for a given idea to take shape.
With a way of meaning,
I pray for its grandeur,
to what an inspiration it can be.
Too many people around us,
insist that we put up with a fuss.
All around us we must,
stand tall to be counted.
As each one of us is
an inspiration,
we can always create
a sensation.
When used directly,
not for any other thing,
except forth for us to bring,
to be ear marked for our thing.
Till someday we go broke,
give us old folk a break.
We are not lost without words,
we are not feeble-minded.
Another reliable idea to make,
with give and take at the helm,
the oldsters will have lots of ideas to heart,
which some they don't wish to part.

*Tinkering Around With Insanity*

**They're ideas and life they
haven't blown,
these will be the greatest stories
ever told,
if you only lend an ear to listen
and be so bold!**

*Nancy Susan Michael*

# In The Darkness

In the darkness where we reside,
floating in a sea forever.
We strive to fight for life,
of which we don't want to stifle.
Fighting for our very lives,
It is the darkness which springs forth life,
Whenever it is their time for them.
We live out in a sea of water,
it is like our own special home.
Just floating in a sea of never ending.
Time and space not being a waste.
It is a new beginning for most of us,
to be in this sea of darkness.
Will be a real treat for the entity,
ready to just grin and bear it all.
Putting a presence on their very soul,
testing their minds for virtual reality.
Our minds go in three D.
Switch over to the calm and serene.
It is not experienced with them yet.
Living in a sea of darkness.
Safe and happy from the world,
without a single care or woe.
Not having a fight off any foe,
not that at the beginning we bare all.
Just for a few privileged souls.
Who seems to want to make merry,
each time one of us is pressured.

## Tinkering Around With Insanity

Into water each of us is nestled,
till each of us were sent.
A message which is meant.
Some of us have wept.
It is the tranquility they seek.
It is certainty not for the meek.
Nor is it for the weak.
It is time to think quick,
forever holding their peace.
It is not done in the East or West,
It is done mostly in the south.
Word of mouth has it that,
if they wish to remain silent,
Floating down towards their aperture.
Neatly tucked away in their own world,
not knowing day by day.
The aperture seems to be expanding.
Putting forth a cosmic energy,
unlike none other.
It is past their capability,
to realize what is going on now.
Onward into things we know,
onto something much more grand.
The aperture is finally opening.
The entity slides further downward,
towards a whole new experience.
One such will be living,
what will it be like?
The aperture is crawling with life.
It is something to see.
Be it you or me,
being born into this world.

*Nancy Susan Michael*

Sure does take an unusual turn,
but it is a good turn.
When a baby cries for the first time,
life which we know it can be very kind,
making it through that aperture
takes strength and might!

## A Guiding Vision

As the soldier steps out
of the plane,
the world around him
seemed tame.
It was well worth a check.
He was a United States Marine,
put there to do his job.
To bother him is to let,
to let feelings of the past sink in.
His ears would be tinny,
after the sounds of the bombs
overhead.
It did not affect the dead.
Message to them I'll send.
It's a tough life,
and you've been through the worse.
I don't want your bubble burst,
but there is no way to
rebuild CA.
As the soldier stepped through the debris,
The earthquake was a lot to see.
The bomb that was dropped,
was just enough stuff,
to make the earth start shaking,
making people quiver at the same time.
The message I'll send,
The world now needs to be on the mend.
The whole world indeed is in trouble,
from what I can see

*Nancy Susan Michael*

on the double.
A love for the human body takes over.
It makes the soldier mad.
He is first saddened by,
how many others hide.
Bad to let rumors fly
when there is war.
When the ink started to flow,
he got up to go,
he did not want any bombs dropped.
He walked on.
He was absolutely stunned,
by what damage a bomb can do.
From his point of view.
The people had no choice too
on whether or not we
can prevent tragic situations
like these.
We all know the score.
that when the bombs started to drop.
He was supposed to foresee,
any people who were,
burying the dead.
Any happy emotions left,
if any,
any people who were
all alone too,
and round them up.
He is also praying,
he will probably have to stay,
to make his own way.
Through all the dirt.

*Tinkering Around With Insanity*

He hadn't been too perky.
Since he'd been praying,
He hadn't had a chance to lay,
on the hard ground,
His breathing is found to be sparse,
When it got dark,
is what scared him.
He could catch a wink,
only if he could find,
a descent place to sleep.
He'd tried the ground,
but only to toss and turn,
he didn't know where or if,
he could ever find a place to sleep.
Most of the night he looked.
He found his place,
under a weeping willow tree,
he was one, lonely person,
but the tree gave him solace.
During the course of the evening,
A vision of Jesus appeared before him.
"Why are you here, soldier?"
"To fid my parents…"
The tree swayed to protect him.
As Jesus was standing there,
"This place is absolutely gone,
with all people killed."
"Come over to my arms,
we'll go to heaven."
"Heaven can't wait," the soldier said,

*Nancy Susan Michael*

"It is time to go on,"
and the weeping willow tree,
will always weep for him.
Jesus came back for him,
and wouldn't let him go.
The soldier will always remember
the day of the Rapture!

Printed in the United States
19121LVS00001B/133-153